Manatees

Victoria Blakemore

Copyright info/picture credits

Cover, NICOLAS LARENTO/AdobeStock; Page 3, Jim P Reid/Pixnio; Page 5, FF16/Pixabay; Page 7, Ryan Hagerty/Pixnio; Page 9, andrewbecks/Pixabay; Pages 10-11, Kanenori/Pixabay; Page 13, kaileighw723/Twenty20; Page 15, Jim P Reid/Pixnio; Page 17, Galen Rathbun/Pixnio; Page 19, Jim P Reid/Pixnio; Page 21, Jim P Reid/Pixnio; Page 23; Doug Perrine/Pixabay; Page 25, Robert K Bonde/Pixnio; Page 27, Jorge E Saliva/Pixnio; Page 29, Keith Ramos/Pixnio; Page 31, ugadawgphotographer/Twenty20; Page 33, NICOLAS LARENTO/AdobeStock

Table of Contents

What Are Manatees?

Manatees are large marine mammals. They are related to elephants.

There are three different kinds of manatees. Their main differences are where they live and their size.

Manatees can be many

shades of gray and brown.

Size

Adult manatees often range in size from eight to thirteen feet long.

Most manatees weigh between 800 and 1,300 pounds when they are fully grown.

Some Florida manatees

have been known to weigh

over 1,600 pounds.

Physical Characteristics

Manatees have a large, flat tail that they use to swim and front flippers that help them steer.

They are usually gray or brown in color. They may also look green. This is because they move to slowly that a plant called algae grows on their skin.

Manatees have short, spiny

whiskers. The whiskers are

thought to help the manatees

feel vibrations. **7**

Habitat

Manatees are found in rivers and water around the **coast**. They prefer water that is warm. Some manatees **migrate** to warmer waters in the winter.

They are usually found in water that isn't too deep. They need to be able to find enough plants to eat.

Range

Manatees are found around

parts of Africa, North America,

and South America.

In the United States, the Florida

manatee is found from

Louisiana to the east coast.

Diet

Manatees are **herbivores**.

They only eat plants.

Their diet is made up of sea grasses, algae, and mangrove leaves. In zoos, they may also eat things like lettuce and banana leaves.

Manatees use their lips to tear

off a piece of a plant and bring

the food to their mouth.

Manatees have strong teeth that help them to break the plants down.

If a manatee loses a tooth, a new tooth will grow in to replace it. They only have molars, which they use to grind their food.

Manatees are often called sea cows because of their slow movements and the way they **graze** on plants.

Communication

Manatees use mainly sound and touch to communicate with other manatees.

They can make sounds such as chirps, whistles, or squeaks. Their sounds are made when they are scared or interacting with other manatees.

Manatees have been seen

nuzzling each other, especially

mothers and calves.

Movement

Manatees are very slow moving. They usually swim less than five miles per hour. They can swim up to fifteen miles per hour for short times.

When they rest, they can stay underwater for about fifteen minutes before they need to surface for air.

Manatees that are swimming

must come to the surface to

breathe every few minutes.

Manatee Life

Manatees are seen alone, in pairs, or in small groups. They can be social or **solitary**.

Manatees that are in groups have been **observed** playing together. They may play follow the leader or ride small currents.

Manatees spend most of their

time resting or eating plants.

Manatee Calves

Manatees usually have one baby. It is called a calf.

The calf is born underwater. The mother may help the calf to the surface to breathe. The calf can swim by itself within about an hour.

Most calves stay with their

mothers for about two years.

Lifespan

In the wild, manatees often live between fifty and sixty years. They have few natural **predators** in the wild.

Manatees sometimes get sick if the weather gets too cold. They can also die from disease and the **toxins** in red tide.

Manatees that live in South

America may have problems

with lakes drying up.

All kinds of manatees are **endangered**. There are not many left in the wild.

The Florida manatee is one of the most endangered marine mammals. In 2015, there were thought to be about 6,300 left in the wild.

Florida manatees are in trouble.

People are trying to help them.

Manatees in Danger

Many manatees are facing habitat loss and destruction. Their habitats are being destroyed and **polluted**.

Manatees are slow-moving and dark in color. They can be hard to see in the water. This makes them **vulnerable** to being hit by boats.

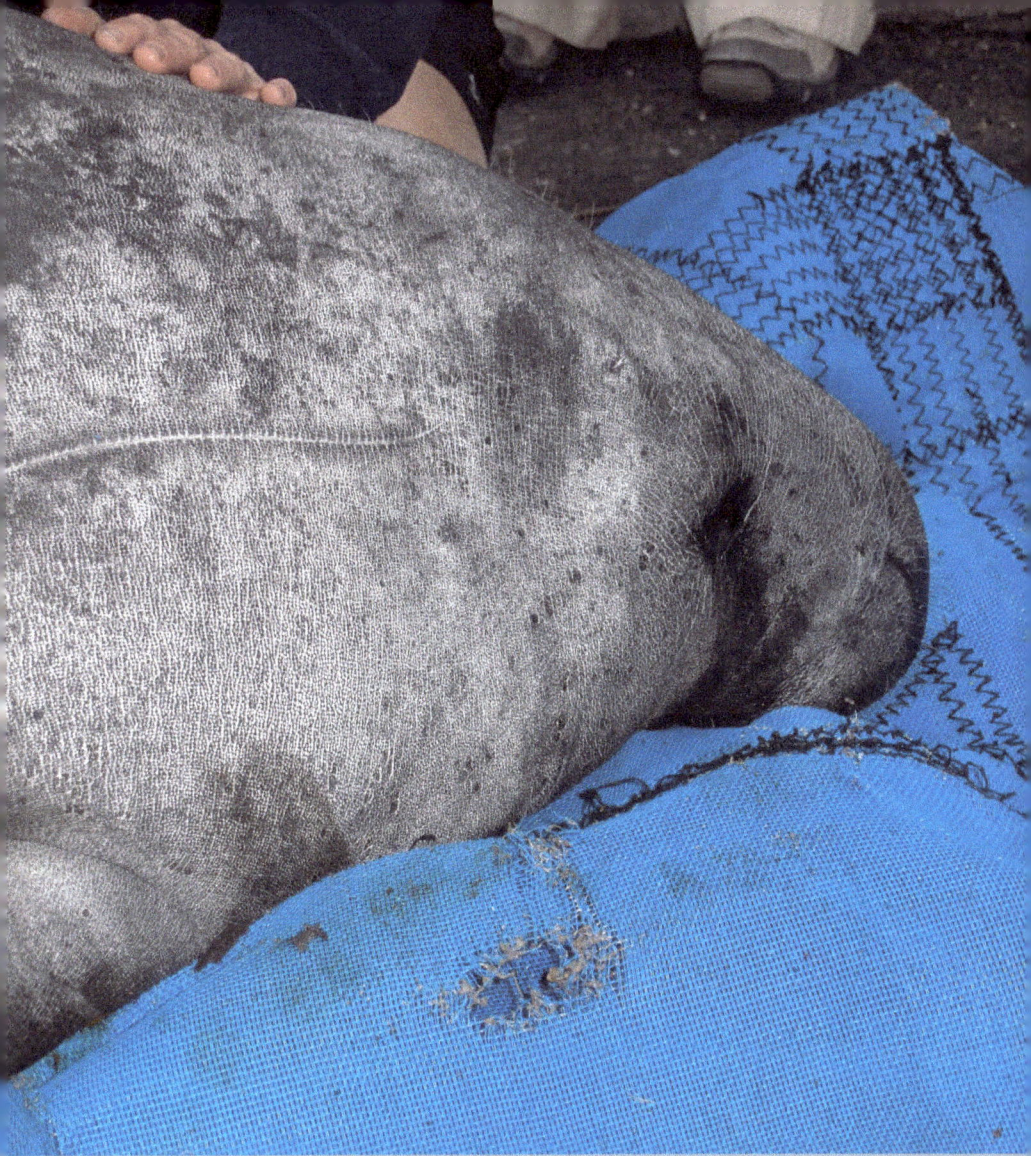

Manatees can also get tangled

up in fishing nets. This can injure

or kill manatees.

Helping Manatees

Many people are trying to help wild manatees. There are laws to protect manatees from habitat loss and boaters.

Manatee zone signs are posted in areas where manatees are known to be. They warn boaters to go slowly and watch for manatees.

MANATEE ZONE
SLOW SPEED
MINIMUM WAKE
OCT 1 THRU APRIL 30

25 MPH

REMAINDER OF YEAR

Some groups help manatees that have been injured by boats or fishing nets. They take care of the manatees until they can be re-released into the wild.

These steps are helping many manatees. The Florida manatee population has been increasing. The hope is that they won't be endangered any more.

Glossary

Coast: the area of land that meets the ocean

Endangered: at risk of becoming extinct

Graze: to feed on growing grass

Herbivore: an animal that eats only plants

Migrate: when an animal travels from one place to another

Observed: seen or noticed

Polluted: harmful to health because of waste or toxins

Predator: an animal that hunts other animals

Solitary: living alone

Toxins: poisonous substances created by plants or animals

Vulnerable: able to be hurt or injured

About the Author

Victoria Blakemore is a first grade

teacher in Southwest Florida with a

passion for reading.

You can visit her at

www.elementaryexplorers.com

Also in This Series

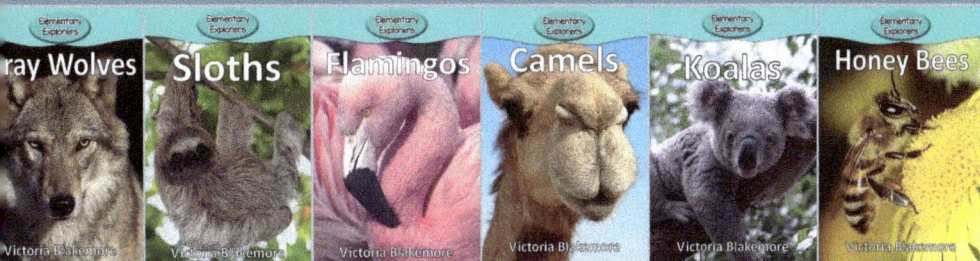

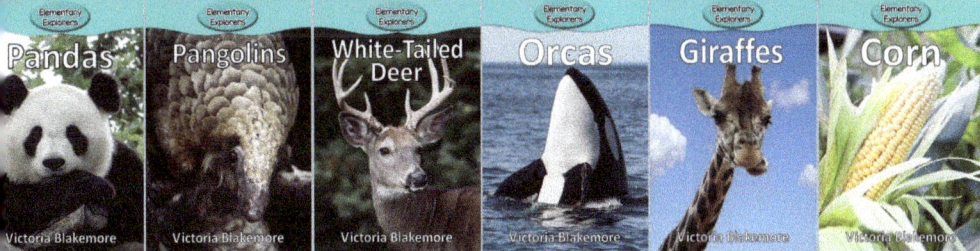

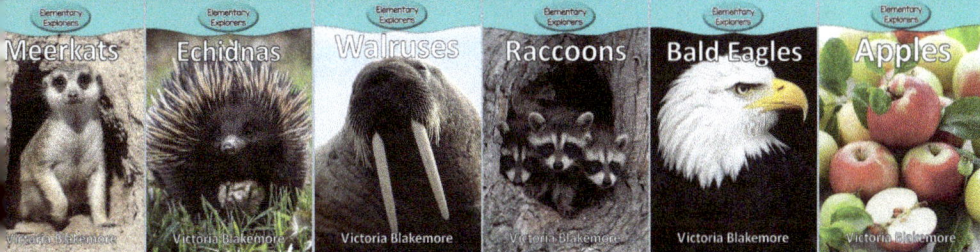

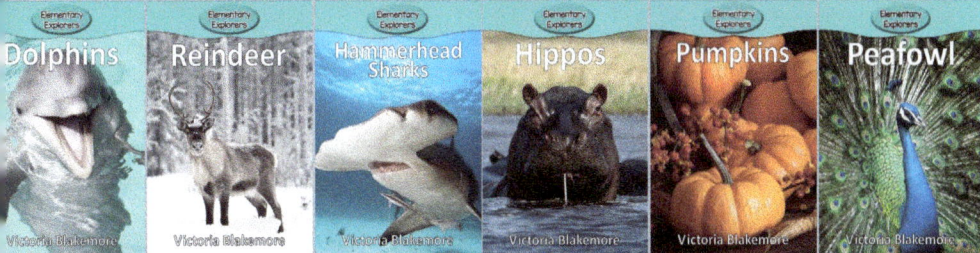

Gray Wolves	Sloths	Flamingos	Camels	Koalas	Honey Bees
Pandas	Pangolins	White-Tailed Deer	Orcas	Giraffes	Corn
Meerkats	Echidnas	Walruses	Raccoons	Bald Eagles	Apples
Arctic Foxes	Red Pandas	Cassowaries	Tigers	Ladybugs	Moose
Beluga Whales	Leopards	Elephants	Jellyfish	Binturongs	Lions
Dolphins	Reindeer	Hammerhead Sharks	Hippos	Pumpkins	Peafowl

Also in This Series

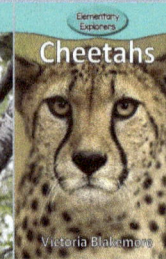

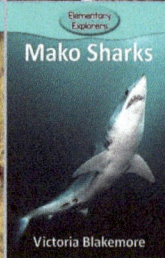

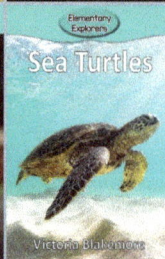

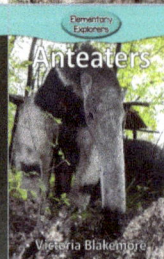

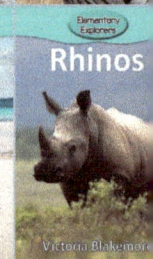

Chameleons — Victoria Blakemore
Florida Panthers — Victoria Blakemore
Aye-Ayes — Victoria Blakemore
Black Bears — Victoria Blakemore
Cheetahs — Victoria Blakemore
Manatee — Victoria Blakemore

Gingerbread — Victoria Blakemore
Polar Bears — Victoria Blakemore
Hot Chocolate — Victoria Blakemore
Orangutans — Victoria Blakemore
Coyotes — Victoria Blakemore
Marshmallow — Victoria Blakemore

Strawberries — Victoria Blakemore
Aardvarks — Victoria Blakemore
Mako Sharks — Victoria Blakemore
Alligators — Victoria Blakemore
Frogs — Victoria Blakemore
Hedgehog — Victoria Blakemore

Brown Bears — Victoria Blakemore
Bongos — Victoria Blakemore
Sea Turtles — Victoria Blakemore
Quokkas — Victoria Blakemore
Muskrats — Victoria Blakemore
Zebras — Victoria Blakemore

Red Foxes — Victoria Blakemore
Ring-Tailed Lemurs — Victoria Blakemore
Platypuses — Victoria Blakemore
Anteaters — Victoria Blakemore
Kangaroos — Victoria Blakemore
Rhinos — Victoria Blakemore

Jaguars — Victoria Blakemore
Wombats — Victoria Blakemore